Animals Change Their Clothes

By JoAnne Nelson • Pictures by Grace Goldberg

MODERN CURRICULUM PRESS

PROJECT DIRECTOR: Judith E. Nayer
COVER DESIGN: Elaine A. Groth

Published by Modern Curriculum Press

Modern Curriculum Press, Inc.
A division of Simon & Schuster
13900 Prospect Road, Cleveland, Ohio 44136

Copyright © 1990 by McClanahan Book Company, Inc. All rights reserved.

This edition is published simultaneously in Canada by
Globe/Modern Curriculum Press, Toronto.

Manufactured in the United States of America. This book or parts thereof may not be reproduced in any form or mechanically stored in any retrieval system without written permission of the publisher.

ISBN 0-8136-4290-6 (STY PK)   ISBN 0-8136-4286-8 (BK)

10 9 8 7 6   94

What will you wear,
little brown snake?
What will you wear in the spring?

A skin that is smooth,
and helps me to move.
That's what I'll wear in the spring.

What will you wear,
little brown snake?
What will you wear in the summer?

A new skin will show,
as I change and I grow.
That's what I'll wear in the summer.

What will you wear,
little brown snake?
What will you wear in the fall?

A new skin that is stronger,
so I can grow longer.
That's what I'll wear in the fall.

What will you wear,
deer of the forest?
What will you wear in the summer?

A light coat of brown,
with spots all around.
That's what I'll wear in the summer.

What will you wear,
deer of the forest?
What will you wear in the fall?

A deep coat of brown,
with my spots nearly gone.
That's what I'll wear in the fall.

What will you wear,
deer of the forest?
What will you wear in the winter?

I'll stand in the snow,
while my new antlers grow.
That's what I'll wear in the winter.

What will you wear,
sly little weasel?
What will you wear in the summer?

A coat of light brown,
helps me hide on the ground.
That's what I'll wear in the summer.

What will you wear,
sly little weasel?
What will you wear in the fall?

My coat will turn white,
while I sleep in the night.
That's what I'll wear in the fall.

What will you wear,
sly little weasel?
What will you wear in the winter?

A coat of pure white,
helps me keep out of sight.
That's what I'll wear in the winter.

NOW . . . how and why do you suppose other animals change their clothes?